JERRY SAVELLE

A Right Mental Attitude

The Doorway to a Successful Life

Unless otherwise stated, all Scripture quotations are taken from *The King James Version* of the Bible.

ISBN 0 - 89274 -159 - 7
Copyright © 1980 by Jerry Savelle
Reprinted 1993
All Rights Reserved

CONTENTS

1. Adorning the Gospel 7
2. Be a Living Epistle - Not a Dead Letter 19
3. The Trial of Your Faith 25
4. Gird Up the Loins of Your Mind 35
5. "Take No Thought" 45
6. A Willingness of Mind 59
7. Bringing Glory to God 67
8. Two Avenues - Faith and Fear 77
9. Become Established in Righteousness 91
10. The Sacrifice of Joy 99
11. Become Strong-Willed 111
12. Greatly Rejoicing - An Aid to a Right Mental Attitude 121

ONE

Adorning The Gospel

•••

*M*any ministers spend a lot of time teaching and preaching on how one is to believe with the heart (spirit). This is very important. How to believe with the heart must be taught. However, I believe that very little has been said on *How To Develop A Right Mental Attitude*. The mind, or the soulish part of man, plays an important part in the Christian's life. That is the reason that the Bible says:

*I beseech you therefore, brethren, by the mercies of God, that ye present your bodies a living sacrifice, holy, acceptable unto God, which is your reasonable service. And be not conformed to this world: but **be ye transformed by the renewing of your mind**, that ye may prove what is that good, and acceptable, and perfect, will of God* (Romans 12:1-2).

There are some things that need to be done where the soul of man is concerned. It is the desire of my heart to teach you, through the inspiration of the Holy Spirit, *How to Develop a Right Mental Attitude*.

A Right Mental Attitude

In the following Scripture passage, the apostle Paul is admonishing Titus to preach sound doctrine. We read in Titus 2:1-15:

But speak thou the things which become sound doctrine:

*That the aged men be **sober**, grave, temperate, sound in faith, in charity, in patience.*

*The aged women likewise, that they be in behaviour as becometh holiness, not false accusers, not given to much wine, teachers of good things; that they may teach the young women to be **sober**, to love their husbands, to love their children, to be discreet, chaste, keepers at home, good, obedient to their own husbands, that the word of God be not blasphemed.*

*Young men likewise exhort to be **sober minded**. In all things showing thyself a pattern of good works: in doctrine shewing uncorruptness, gravity, sincerity, sound speech, that cannot be condemned; that he that is of the contrary part may be ashamed, having no evil thing to say of you.*

Exhort servants to be obedient unto their

own masters, and to please them well in all things; not answering again; not purloining, but shewing all good fidelity; that they may ADORN THE DOCTRINE OF GOD our Saviour in all things.

*For the grace of God that bringeth salvation hath appeared to all men, teaching us that, denying ungodliness and worldly lusts, we should live **soberly**, righteously, and godly, in this present world; looking for that blessed hope, and the glorious appearing of the great God and our Saviour Jesus Christ; who gave himself for us, that he might redeem us from all iniquity, and purify unto himself a peculiar people, zealous of good works.*

These things speak, and exhort, and rebuke with all authority. Let no man despise thee.

You will notice that Paul covered every person that one can think of in these scriptures: men, women, husbands, wives, children, and servants. He emphasizes the fact that the older men are to be temperate and sound in faith. The aged women are to behave as becomes holiness. In other words, they are to live a holy life. They are to be teachers of good things, to exhort the

A Right Mental Attitude

young women to be sober minded, and to have sound speech that cannot be condemned.

The Phillips Translation of the Bible says, "That your speech should be unaffected and above criticism, so that your opponent may feel ashamed at finding nothing which will discredit you" (v. 8). I like that translation: ...*your opponent may feel ashamed at finding nothing which will discredit you.* That goes for Satan, too! Satan is our adversary. Our opponent will be ashamed, and he will find nothing by which he can discredit us.

If your speech is God's words, words of power, then your opponent can find nothing in your speech whereby he can trap or snare you.

Please read verse 10 again: "Not purloining, but shewing all good fidelity; *that they may adorn the doctrine of God our Saviour in all things.*" The word "adorn" means "to beautify; to decorate; to make attractive." Paul is saying that if the people will receive the instructions and do them, they will beautify, decorate, and make the gospel attractive to lost people.

You may adorn your body. You wear nice

clothes, and you look good. You comb your hair and make yourself attractive. You want to look good and presentable. There is nothing wrong with that. You may drive a nice automobile, and there is nothing wrong with your having a nice automobile. You may keep your house adorned; and when people come to see you, they are impressed because your house looks attractive and nice. The point I am making is this: *Many Christians do much about adorning their bodies, their automobiles, or their homes, but they do not even attempt to follow Paul's instructions that will adorn the gospel of Christ.* Paul wants Christians to make the gospel of Jesus Christ attractive to the world.

You Can Beautify The Gospel

It's no wonder that the world has not wanted to be like most Christians. They look at many Christians and think, *Oh, they look so sad and beggarly.* Why? Because they do not see Christians living in victory. But, thank God, there is a better way. If you will start acting on the Word, you will not live in defeat.

Jesus said, *If a man love me, he will keep my words; and my Father will love him, and we will come unto him, and make our abode with him* (John 14:23). I want you to know that when Jesus of Nazareth moves in with you, He will start making things better around where you live. He will teach you how to get out of poverty, and He will teach you how to enjoy prosperity.

The reason that the world has not wanted to have anything to do with Christians is because we have not made the gospel beautiful. We have made it look like something dreadful. The only thing that they might have noticed is that the only difference between them and us is that they are going to hell, and we are going to heaven. Just going to heaven is not what beautifies the gospel. That is a part of it, but that is not all of it. There is much more to Christianity than just escaping hell. I encourage you to escape hell, but let's enjoy ALL that was paid for at Calvary.

Be Sober Minded

Paul lists several things in the second chapter of the book of Titus that will adorn the gospel. I am not going to instruct you in all of those areas that he mentions. But there is one particular principle with which I want to deal. We will read verse six again; "Young men likewise exhort to

Adorning the Gospel

be sober minded." You realize that Paul directed this to the young men, but I believe that if God wants young men to be sober minded, then it is pleasing to Him that old men be sober minded as well. And if He wants old men to be sober minded, then surely He wants old women and young women to also be sober minded. As you read that entire chapter, you can see that some of the things do not apply to me, and they obviously cannot fit you. How can I obey my husband? I don't have one! Some of them do not apply to every individual, but some of them overlap one another. Therefore, if God wants the one person to be *sober minded*, He wants you to be *sober minded*.

What is being *sober minded*?

The center cross-reference in my Bible says that **to be sober minded is to be discreet**. I have spent some time studying this subject in other translations of the Bible, and I believe that **Paul is saying that to be sober minded is to have a right mental attitude**. He is saying that a right mental attitude is one of the things that adorns the gospel.

Failing to have a right mental attitude is

A Right Mental Attitude

another reason that the world hasn't wanted to have anything to do with Christians. Most Christians' mental attitude about life has been negative. They have had such a poor, low mental attitude about life that sinners can see nothing in them that is desirable. Many Christians portray this idea: "If I just bear up under these problems like a good little trooper, that will impress somebody. No! That doesn't impress anybody. It is when you become a "good little trooper" and *overcome the circumstances* that come against you that it is impressive.

Sinners bear up under circumstances. I know some very strong-willed sinners. They have learned how to become strong-willed where their businesses are concerned. They couldn't care less if you are just bearing up under the problem. And if you say, "One of these days it will be worth it all. It will be better on the other side," that does not impress the sinner. *If the gospel will not work against problems that people encounter today, then they are not interested in it.*

Yes, I am excited about going to heaven, but that is not all the gospel provides. I still have to live on the earth in this life time. And if the gospel cannot provide a way to live above the beggarly elements of the world and a way to live above the trials and problems that man experiences, then I am not really too interested in the sweet by-and-by. I am not saying that we should belittle heaven. I thank God for heaven and for the ability to spend eternity with our Lord and Savior Jesus Christ, but let's not get so heavenly minded that we forget about our responsibilities on earth.

When a sinner can look at a Christian and see that he has a right mental attitude about life, about adversity, about circumstances, about trials, and about lack and shortages, then the gospel will look attractive to him.

TWO

Be A Living Epistle - Not A Dead Letter

●●●

*I*t was because somebody made the gospel attractive that caused me to turn my back on sin. All of those preachers who came to my hometown telling me to be a Christian and talking about "poor old me" did not impress me at all. It was when somebody came and showed me how to get out of the mess that I was in by acting on God's Word that caused me to desire to allow God to have full control of my life.

Somebody came along, and preached some *good new*s! He not only taught me how to have faith in my heart, but he caused me to realize the importance of having a right mental attitude about life.

Positive Thinking Alone Is Not Enough

Now, let me say this to you: *Faith is a spiritual force*. Faith resides in the human spirit. However, faith will produce a right mental attitude.

A *right mental attitude* is not *wishful think-*

A Right Mental Attitude

ing. A right mental attitude is having a positive expectancy daily.

Many people talk about the *power of positive thinking.* I am not dealing with that. Although, when you have faith in your heart and the Word of God abiding abundantly in you, it will cause you to *think positively.* All of the promises of God are in Him, "Yea and amen." You cannot become any more positive than that. *Positive thinking alone is not enough.* There are some people in the world today who have become very successful through the *power of positive thinking.* But if they are not thinking on the Word of God, then their positive thinking will be limited in what it can produce.

God's Word is eternal. When you get the Word of God in your heart, you will find that it will also change the way you think. The reason that most Christians have not had a right mental attitude is because they have not spent enough time meditating God's Word.

When we develop a right mental attitude, we can awake each day with a positive expectancy of God moving in our behalf. That is what adorns the gospel of Christ!

Be A Living Epistle - Not a Dead Letter

The apostle Paul said, *Ye are our epistle written in our hearts, known and read of all men* (2 Corinthians 3:2). What does he mean by this? You are the New Testament walking in the flesh. **The world is reading you by your actions, by your words, and by what you do**. If you are not doing anything that adorns the gospel of God, then you are a *dead letter*, and who enjoys reading *dead letters*?

As you get into God's Word and let that Word get into your heart, you will become a *living epistle*. *You will adorn the gospel*. This is what causes others to want Jesus in their lives like He is in yours.

THREE

The Trial Of Your Faith

•••

*F*aith is a spiritual force, residing in your heart, that will produce a right mental attitude. A right mental attitude is one of the things the apostle Paul said makes the gospel attractive.

A *right mental attitude* is profitable when a problem comes against you.

Blessed be the God and Father of our Lord Jesus Christ, which according to his abundant mercy hath begotten us again unto a lively hope by the resurrection of Jesus Christ from the dead.

To an inheritance incorruptible, and undefiled, and that fadeth not away, reserved in heaven for you, who are kept by the power of God through faith unto salvation ready to be revealed in the last time.

Wherein ye greatly rejoice, though now for a season, if need be, ye are in heaviness through manifold temptations; that the trial of your faith, being much more precious than of gold

A Right Mental Attitude

that perisheth, though it be tried with fire, might be found unto praise and honour and glory at the appearing of Jesus Christ...

Wherefore gird up the loins of your mind, be sober, and hope to the end for the grace that is to be brought unto you at the revelation of Jesus Christ (1 Peter 1:3-7, 13).

Peter is talking about the trial of our faith. *Trials of our faith* literally mean "problems, adverse circumstances, and pressures." When it appears, in the natural, that nothing is going well, then there is pressure, there is a tendency to compromise and a tendency to lean towards the natural rather than to put your total trust in what the Word of God says.

God Is Not The Author Of Trials and Tests

Satan (**not God**) is the author of problems, trials, and tests. He comes immediately to steal the Word of God out of one's heart. (Mark 4:14-20.) It does not bring glory to God when you are being tested if you fold up, compromise, and let the devil defeat you. The thing that brings glory to God is when you endure. **To endure means to overcome**.

Shadrach, Meshach, And Abednego Endured Trials By Overcoming Them

An excellent example of somebody enduring trials, temptations, and problems is given in the third chapter of Daniel. These three young Hebrew men had the kind of endurance that brings glory to God. When they came out of that fiery furnace, they were not burned, beat down, beggarly, or helpless. In reality, the trial of their faith had no power over them. There wasn't even a singed hair on their heads. And they did not have the smell of smoke on them. They came out of there bringing honor and glory to God.

Why?

Because they went into that furnace with a right mental attitude. They did not go in there saying, "Oh, dear God, why is this happening to me? It seems like every time I make a decision to go for God, I get burned." Before they were ever shoved into that furnace, they said, "We will not bow our knee; we will not serve your god. Our God will deliver us. He is able. And if we go into the furnace, He is able to deliver us" (author's paraphrase). They were so positive about this that they knew God would deliver them regardless of the circumstances.

They left the door wide open to God. God could do it any way He wanted. They were saying, "It makes no difference whether or not we go into the furnace; we will not serve your god. We will not bow our knee; our God will deliver us. It makes no difference how we approach this trial; our God will deliver us." They had a right mental attitude, praise God!

The Words They Spoke Were Spawned From Faith

You should realize that the words Shadrach, Meshach, and Abednego spoke were the product of their faith - faith in the covenant; faith in their God to deliver them. As they spoke words of faith, they also expressed that they had a right mental attitude. *Their right mental attitude played an important part in their deliverance.*

When Peter was talking about the trial of your faith, he said that the thing that would bring

The Trial of Your Faith

glory and honor to God is that **you come out of the trial a winner** - not beaten down and beggarly, but a winner. **The way that you can come out of a trial a winner is by having faith in your heart, confidence in the Word of God, and a right mental attitude**. In 1 Peter 1:13, he was saying, "When you are in the midst of a trial, you must gird up the loins of your mind; be sober, and develop a right mental attitude" (author's paraphrase).

The worst time to have a wrong or negative mental attitude is when you are under pressure. As long as everything is going well, anyone can have a right mental attitude about life. If you are not experiencing a problem or are not under pressure, then it is easy for you to make strong statements of faith. But when a problem comes along, then you find out what is in your heart and if your attitude is right.

Somebody said, "Well, God must use those things to find out where we really stand." No, God doesn't have to use tests and trials to find out where you really stand. You are not hiding anything from Him. He knows where you stand without any kind of pressure on you.

A Right Mental Attitude

The Bible says, "For the word of God is quick, and powerful, and sharper than any twoedged sword, piercing even to the dividing asunder of soul and spirit, and of the joints and marrow, and is a discerner of the thoughts and intents of the heart. Neither is there any creature that is not manifest in his sight; but *all things are naked and opened unto the eyes of him with whom we have to do*" (Hebrews 4:12-13).

God knows your heart; He knows what you believe. And He doesn't have to send some kind of test or trial to find out whether or not you believe Him. He knows how you will respond; He knows how you will act, and He knows what you are going to say.

The devil is the one who doesn't always know where you stand. He is the one who wants to send you through the fiery furnace to see how you will respond. He doesn't know what you will do until he puts pressure on you. And even then, thank God, you do not have to yield to his pressure. You can keep the devil guessing all the time. Instead of you being the one who is always under pressure, you can put the pressure on him. How? By resisting him with the Word, your faith, and a right mental attitude.

The Trial of Your Faith

First Corinthians 2:14-15 says, *But the natural man receiveth not the things of the Spirit of God: for they are foolishness unto him: neither can he know them, because they are spiritually discerned. But he that is spiritual judgeth all things, yet he himself is judged of no man.*

Paul is saying that a spiritual man is judged of no one. Again, God does not have to send you through any test or trial to find out what you believe. He knows the intents of your heart. But the devil does not - not until you act; not until you talk; not until you respond to the pressure he brings against you. **Keep Satan in the dark; then, when it is time to fight, fight the good fight of faith and win!**

FOUR

Gird Up The Loins Of Your Mind

•••

Wherefore gird up the loins of your mind, be sober, and hope to the end for the grace that is brought unto you at the revelation of Jesus Christ (1 Peter 1:13).

When Peter said, *Gird up the loins of your mind*, he was actually saying that *a right mental attitude is important.* A right mental attitude is of the utmost importance when you are experiencing trouble. That part of the body (the loins) is not in the mind. Peter used that phrase metaphorically.

Paul also used the term *loins* in his letter to the Ephesians. He said, *Wherefore take unto you the whole armour of God, that ye may be able to withstand in the evil day, and having done all, to stand. **Stand therefore, having your loins girt about with truth**, and having on the breastplate of righteousness* (Ephesianas 6:13-14). Paul was talking about putting on the whole armor of God that we might stand against the wiles of the devil.

The Amplified Bible states those verses this

way: "Therefore put on God's complete armor, that you may be able to resist and stand your ground on the evil day (of danger), and having done all (the crisis demands), to stand (firmly in your place). Stand therefore - hold your ground - having tightened the belt of truth around your loins." Verse 11 of *The Amplified Bible* says, "...that you may be able to successfully stand up against (all) the strategies and the deceits of the devil."

The loins is that part of the body that contains strength and power. When Peter used that physical part of the body as a figure of speech, he was implying a region of strength and power in the mind.

Willpower Alone Is Not Enough

Peter and Paul are implying that there is a region of strength and creative power in the mind. **The power that is released from the mind is called "willpower."** It is evidence that **willpower is one of the things - along with faith in God's Word - that makes the gospel attractive**.

The problem is that many Christians have

Gird Up the Loins of Your Mind

no *willpower*, and when trouble comes to them, they fall aside. Please understand: willpower alone is not enough. Faith must be mixed with willpower. **A right mental attitude is created by faith in God's Word.**

Meditate The Word

Most Christians spend a lot of time reading their Bibles, but many of them have a negative mental attitude about everything. The reason that their mental attitude is not right is because *they are only reading* the Bible, and they are not meditating upon the Word. The Bible stresses the importance of meditation in God's Word. *Meditation on the Word is literally "digesting God's Word in your mind." And as you digest the Word, it will drop down into your heart (spirit) and lodge there.*

What you do with your mind is important. Let's not leave the mind out. It plays a very important part in victorious Christian living. The loins of the mind is the region of strength and creative power. The word *gird* implies, "Get ready to do something that may be difficult or demand strength." When Peter said, "Gird up the loins of your mind," he was saying that when

A Right Mental Attitude

you are experiencing a problem, that is the moment you need to gird up the loins of your mind. You are not only to draw from the faith in your heart, but you must also begin to develop a right mental attitude about the problem, just as the three young Hebrew men did.

It is of utmost importance that you stand on the authority of God's Word, and that you absolutely demand that all negativism depart from your mind when you approach a trial or an adverse circumstance. If you approach the trial with a wrong mental attitude, it is likely that you will not release any faith. You will not expect to win. You will come out defeated and discouraged.

When you gird up the loins of your mind, you are preparing yourself mentally for anything that may come against you. The faith in your heart will then put you over and bring victory. (1 John 5:1-4). You will think positively about the situation you are about to encounter. Your thinking will be derived from what you have found in God's Word. You are well equipped, both mentally and spiritually, for anything and everything.

Your Heart And Mind Must Be In Agreement

Let's suppose that you are approaching a financial crisis, and you have all the symptoms of lack. You can have symptoms of lack just as you can have symptoms of a cold.

When the symptom of lack comes to you, if you have been meditating in the Word of God, the first thing that will come up out of your heart will be faith. If your mind is renewed (Romans 12:2) and you have a right mental attitude, you will automatically think: "What does the Word say about this?" Did you notice that your mind and your heart were in agreement?

Your mind is a computer, and it will begin to select the scriptures that you have stored up concerning prosperity. You then will begin to confess those scriptures and your heart will supply the faith to cause them to come to pass. The result will be **victory**!

Instead of your heart saying, "My God meets my needs according to His riches in glory by Christ Jesus", and your head screaming, "But this is too big," you will approach that financial

A Right Mental Attitude

problem with a right mental attitude. Your mind and your heart will be in agreement. You will be standing on the authority of God's Word. Your faith and a right mental attitude will work together to overcome the situation.

A crisis is nothing but an instrument of Satan to try your faith. And right at that moment, when you are entering into that situation, you need to gird up the loins of your mind. You are not only drawing from faith in your heart, but you must be strong-willed. Jesus did this in the Garden of Gethsemane. He applied the faith in His heart when He willfully submitted himself to do what was necessary at Calvary. You will notice that His mind also played a part in it. He said, "Not my will be done, but thine." Jesus became very *strong-willed* in this. When He made up His mind that "it is going to be the will of God and nothing else," nothing could stop Him. He was not only drawing from faith in His heart, but He had a right mental attitude about what He was about to face.

When Peter tried to talk Him out of it, Jesus could not be moved. He said, "Get thee behind me, Satan." When Jesus made up His mind to do it, there was nothing that could stop Him. He became *strong-willed*. Can you see what an aid this is to your faith?

In the midst of a trial you need to gird up the loins of your mind; get ready to do something difficult. Reach into that region of strength that will cause your faith to become unwavering.

FIVE

Take No Thought

•••

*I*saiah 26:3 says, *Thou will keep him in perfect peace, whose mind is stayed on thee; because he trusteth in thee.* You will notice that God has given us a promise, but we must meet His condition. The promise is: *He will keep you in perfect peace.* The condition is ...*if your mind is stayed on Him.* The mind plays a vital part in your being kept in perfect peace.

Some people may think that I am talking about *mind power.* No! I am not talking about *mind power.* I am talking about the power of God's Word working in a faith-filled heart and a renewed mind.

You should know that you are to be sober minded and that you should develop a *right mental attitude.* As you do this, you will begin to learn how to approach every situation in your life without worry or fear.

In the following Scripture passage, Luke 12:22-32, Jesus teaches us that Christians are not to take any thought (worry) about the material necessities of life:

A Right Mental Attitude

Therefore I say unto you, Take no thought for your life, what ye shall eat; neither for the body, what ye shall put on. The life is more than meat, and the body is more than raiment.

Consider the ravens; for they neither sow nor reap; which neither have storehouse nor barn; and God feedeth them; how much more are ye better than the fowls?

And which of you with taking thought can add to his stature one cubit? If ye then be not able to do that thing which is least, why take ye thought for the rest?

Consider the lilies how they grow: they toil not, they spin not; and yet I say unto you, that Solomon in all his glory was not arrayed like one of these.

If then God so clothe the grass, which is to day in the field, and tomorrow is cast into the oven; how much more will he clothe you, O ye of little faith?

And seek not ye what ye shall eat, or what ye shall drink, neither be ye of doubtful mind. For all these things do the nations of the world seek after: and your Father knoweth that ye have need of these things.

But rather seek ye the kingdom of God; and all these things shall be added unto you. Fear not, little flock; for it is your Father's good pleasure to give you the kingdom.

Jesus is telling us how to live a "worry-free" life. He says that we do not have to live in suspense or have a doubtful mind. We can live with a positive attitude, knowing that God will take care of us if we will simply seek *first* the kingdom of God. If we will do this, then it pleases the Father to give us the kingdom (v. 32).

"...Neither Be Of Doubtful Mind ...Fear Not..."

The things that Jesus said belong to us are the very things that Satan tries to get us to worry about the most. He tries to make us doubt that God will ever give us the necessities of life. Just before Jesus left the earth, He said, "Lo, I am with you always." He also said, "I will never leave you or forsake you." In spite of what Jesus promised, many Christians still suffer from insecurity, which is one of the greatest of all fears.

A Right Mental Attitude

Satan wants the Christians to be insecure, and he attacks them with everything imaginable in order to cause them to worry and fret.

Deuteronomy 8:18 says, *But thou shalt remember the Lord thy God: for it is he that giveth thee power to get wealth, that he may establish his covenant which he sware unto thy fathers, as it is this day.* Yet, many people still greatly fear that they are not going to have enough to meet their needs.

Fear is a spiritual force that will destroy a right mental attitude. That is the reason Jesus said, "Take no thought...fear not...Be not of doubtful mind." He said, "Don't you know that your heavenly Father loves you and will take care of you? There is no need for you to worry about anything. Oh, ye of little faith" (author's paraphrase).

If Satan can create fear in your heart and cause you to have a wrong mental attitude, he can stop you from receiving the blessings of God. Satan comes to kill, to steal, and to destroy. Fear is what opens the door of your life for him.

In verse 32, Jesus said, *"Fear not little*

flock; for it is your Father's good pleasure to give you the kingdom." Fear is the parent of three great diseases that infect the human mind. *Apathy, inertia, and procrastination* are brought on by fear. *Apathy* means "becoming indifferent, having a lack of motivation." *Inertia* is "inactivity and passiveness." *Procrastination* means "to hold back and to put off until later."

Jesus said, "Take no thought." Why does He say this?

Somebody said, "Well, I just can't do that. I can't live on this earth without thinking about my needs, without thinking about what I am going to wear, and without thinking about food and shelter." He didn't say, "Don't think!" He is implying that we shouldn't worry about anything.

Jesus is talking about *doubtful thinking* here - or *negative thinking*. He said, "Take no thought for these things for your heavenly Father knoweth that you have need of them." And He said, "Fear not ...it is your Father's good pleasure to give you the kingdom."

A Right Mental Attitude

When Satan Stoked The Furnace For Me

A few years ago, I was just going along doing what I felt God wanted me to do and having a good time, when all of a sudden it looked as though the bottom had dropped out. I know that Satan has not learned any new tricks, and he has probably pulled the same thing on you. But as I was doing what God had instructed me to do, I realized that my finances had stopped. There were internal problems in my organization. In fact, there was a lot of strife. The next thing I knew, I was approximately $20,000 in debt. I had been paying my way and believing God to "owe no man anything but to love him." Everything had been working fine, and God had honored His Word all the way. Then it happened! I cried, "Dear God! I have $20,000 worth of bills, and I don't have enough to pay them!"

The devil hit me with this: "You ugly thing! You go out there and preach that God meets your needs, and you can't even pay your bills. Why don't you just go and hide somewhere and just shut down this ministry?"

"Take No Thought"

I was tempted to call Brother Kenneth Copeland and ask him if I could have my old job back. Oh, it would have been easy to do that. The blaze was burning; Satan was about to shove me in the furnace, and it was hot. I wanted to play around in self-pity and say, "Bless God, I have been out there preaching the Gospel; I have been faithful; I have travelled this United States from one end to the other; I have driven all night; I have flown every airline in the country. I have preached three and four services a day, seven days a week when it was necessary. God! Why did this happen to me?"

You know that kind of talk doesn't impress God at all, and it certainly doesn't help your matters, either. Somebody said, "Yes, God caused that to happen to you so you would learn your lesson."

No! The reason I was in that trial was that I had opened the door to it myself. I had been so busy that I had gotten out of fellowship with God's Word, and it made me a prime target for Satan's attack.

So, there I was in a $20,000 furnace, and it was hot. I did not understand why it was

A Right Mental Attitude

happening to me. I thought that I had been doing all the right things and that everybody loved me. I had no enemies who would want to see me in a situation like that. It started playing on my mind. And the more I thought about the situation, the more I realized that I was not doing what Peter said to do.

Peter said when you are in that kind of situation to "gird up the loins of your mind." I had been letting my mind run away with me. I sat there in that $20,000 furnace and thought *negatively*.

I have been in the Word of God since 1969. I am not a novice. I knew what the Word said to do. And I knew what the Word said would happen if I would be a doer of the Word. But at that moment, I wanted to just play around in self-pity and do nothing. That caused the disease of *apathy*. I felt indifferent about it. I couldn't have cared less at that moment if I won or lost.

I want you to know that at that moment I felt very indifferent about the gospel. I did not care if anybody got saved. I did not care if anybody got healed, and I did not care if anybody got delivered. In fact, I did not really care if I got delivered. The only thing I can remember saying was what John said in Revelation: "Come quickly, Lord Jesus."

Somebody might say, "Oh, Brother Jerry, you shouldn't tell people those things." Listen, I believe in being honest with people. Someone may be having these same thoughts, and my testimony could be the inspiration they need to be delivered.

I thought, *Bless God! I have dedicated my life to God. I am doing everything that I know the gospel tells me to do, and then I get stuck with this.* That was wrong thinking. That did not line up with the Word of God.

The next thing that happened in my mind was the disease of *inertia*, or *inactivity*. I did not do anything; I did not want to talk to anyone; and I did not want to read my Bible. I did not want to do what I knew I should be doing.

I was in the midst of a trial. And I was not doing what I was supposed to be doing.

When you are in the midst of a trial is not the time to run from the Word. But you see, some-

A Right Mental Attitude

times we allow ourselves to learn things the hard way. And that was what I was doing in that situation. It was not God's fault. It was Jerry's fault. God was more than willing to teach me, in His Word, how to avoid a $20,000 furnace. But I chose to do it the hard way.

Then came the third mental disease: *procrastination*. I thought, *Tomorrow, I will get into the Word of God and get out of this mess. I know I can get out of this, but I am just not going to do anything now. I guess I'll just burn some more.*

Can you see the danger of these three terrible diseases? They cause you to have a wrong attitude. And you may say, "It makes no difference what I do. It won't work anyway."

The devil doesn't play fair, and that is the reason Jesus said, "Take no thought ...Don't be of doubtful mind ...Fear not ..." He is telling you and me how to avoid those $20,000 furnaces.

After I had *cooked* a while, I finally decided, "Praise God, I know better than this." And I got into the Word. I picked myself up by the ear and said, "Jerry Savelle, you are not a failure.

Failures are not *God-made*. And you are not going to fail."

The fact that I had failed once before, as a businessman, started coming to my thinking. Satan kept feeding me this: "You failed in that business, you jerk, and you are going to fail in this."

I said, "NO! When I was in that business I was not a Believer, but I am now. I am a partaker of His divine nature, and it is not God's nature to fail. Praise God." I pulled myself up out of that furnace and began to feed my inner man the Word. I began to gird up the loins of my mind. I began to draw from that creative power in God's Word. I spoke the Word to that $20,000 furnace and I want you to know I came out of it.

Oh, yes, it was difficult. It looked as though I would never get out. But I want you to know, praise God, today I am out! And I'll never go through that furnace again. Do you see what I am saying? A right mental attitude about the necessities of life is important.

Jesus said, **Take no thought**.

SIX

A Willingness Of Mind

●●●

*T*he Bible talks about a *willingness of mind*. **A willingness of mind produces action**. The majority of the time, all actions are preceded by thoughts - unless one acts by instinct. A person will think about something and then do it.

That is the reason that God stressed to Joshua, *This book of the law shall not depart out of thy mouth; but thou shalt meditate therein day and night, that thou mayest observe to do according to all that is written therein: for then thou shalt make thy way prosperous, and then thou shalt have good success* (Joshua 1:8). He was saying that the meditation should come before action. The thought precedes the action. In other words, He told him to get into the Word, talk the Word, think about the Word, meditate the Word, and have a *willingness of mind* to do the Word.

David told his son Solomon, *And thou, Solomon my son, know thou the God of thy father, and serve him with a perfect heart and a willing mind ...if thou seek him he will be found of thee; but if thou forsake him, he will cast thee*

A Right Mental Attitude

off for ever (1 Chronicles 28:9). You are to serve God with a perfect heart and a willing mind.

In Second Corinthians 8:10-12, Paul was talking about giving and receiving. But he talked about the *willingness* to do it first. *And herein I give my advice; for this is expedient for you, who have begun before, not only to do, but also to be forward a year ago. Now therefore perform the doing of it: that as there was a readiness to will, so there may be a performance also out of that which ye have. For if there be first a willing mind, it is accepted according to that a man hath, and not according to that he hath not.*

Paul was talking about a willingness of mind when he said to the Philippians, *But I rejoiced in the Lord greatly, that now at the last your care of me hath flourished again; wherein ye were also careful, but ye lacked opportunity* (Philippians 4:10). Paul was saying, "You were willing, but you lacked opportunity."

A willingness of mind is important. For example, when someone prays over the offering in a service, God will speak to your heart and tell you what to do. He does not speak to your head.

However, if you do not have a willingness of mind, you will not obey what God tells your heart to do.

Isaiah says, *If ye be willing and obedient, ye shall eat the good of the land* (Isaiah 1:19). There is no limitation to a man who has faith in his heart, a right mental attitude, and a willingness of mind. He will eat the good of the land.

Be Willing To Be Successful

If you are a doer of the Word, you are willing to act. In other words, you are prepared to do the Word. The Bible says that a doer of the Word shall be blessed in his deed. He shall eat of the good of the land. You must have a willingness of mind; that is when the action comes.

Many times the airlines put magazines in the seats for the passengers to read. I have noticed that often many of them have some kind of *get rich quick deal*. I have read about somebody who made a lot of money and then has tried to explain his secret. The secret is always in bold print. It will jump out of the page at you. I read one article that said something like this: *You've got to be willing to be successful*. Then it said,

A Right Mental Attitude

The man that only does what he is paid to do, is only paid for what he does. In other words, if all you do is what you are paid to do, and you are not *willing* to do more, then all you will ever get paid for is what you do. That is exactly what Isaiah said: "If you are willing and obedient, you will eat the good of the land."

Many Christians want to do just what they can get by with; they don't like responsibility. I have noticed that those who carry the greatest loads are also the ones who seem to be the most blessed. Why? The reason is because they are willing. Many people want to be successful, but they are not *willing* to do what is necessary to obtain success. **Those who carry the heaviest loads reap the greatest rewards.**

Once Jesus' disciples were arguing with one another about "Who is the chiefest?" Jesus answered them, "The chiefest is the one who is the servant to all." When you have a willingness of mind to be servant to all, then you are going to carry the heaviest loads. But the one who carries the heaviest loads is going to reap the greatest rewards.

Peter proved that. He became a servant to every man, and God made him a chief apostle.

Satan's Aim Is To Destroy A Willingness of Mind

What does Satan do? He causes fear in your heart. He causes you to fear in order to destroy a *willingness of mind*. If he can do this, he can keep you from laying hold upon what God says is yours now.

Faith in your heart, a right mental attitude, and a *willingness of mind* are some of the ingredients for overcoming trials. Begin to develop then **now**.

SEVEN

Bringing Glory To God

●●●

Blessed be the God and Father of our Lord Jesus Christ, which according to his abundant mercy hath begotten us again unto a lively hope by the resurrection of Jesus Christ from the dead.

To an inheritance incorruptible, and undefiled, and that fadeth not away, reserved in heaven for you, who are kept by the power of God through faith unto salvation ready to be revealed in the last time.

Wherein ye greatly rejoice, though now for a season, if need be, ye are in heaviness through manifold temptations (1 Peter 1:3-6).

Notice in the above Scripture passage, Peter said *ye are in heaviness through manifold temptations*. He goes on to say in verse 7, *That the trial of your faith, being much more precious than of gold that perisheth, though it be tried with fire, might be found unto praise and honour and glory at the appearing of Jesus Christ.* If you have been under pressure or in a trial, it was brought on by Satan. He brings heaviness -

A Right Mental Attitude

heaviness of spirit, heaviness of mind, and many times, heaviness physically.

The first thing that you should realize is this: **It is important that you do not blame the trial on God**. God is not the author of trials. The trial is brought on by Satan. Jesus said that once the Word is sown in a man's heart, Satan comes immediately to steal it and to take it away. He also told us that there are five major avenues that Satan will use to do this to us: afflictions, persecutions, the cares of this world, the lust of other things, and the deceitfulness of riches (Mark 4:14-20).

Satan is the tempter; he is the one who brings condemnation to you. He is the one that brings the heaviness, not God.

The apostle Paul describes it this way in verse 7: "...though it be tried with fire..." I described it in a previous chapter concerning the young Hebrew men in the fiery furnace. Many times the trials that you are involved in feel like you are on fire or in a fiery furnace.

God wants you to know that you can endure anything Satan brings against you. And if you will follow the instructions in His Word, you will come out on the other side of that trial like Shadrach, Meshach, and Abednego did: untouched, unharmed and totally protected. That is when you bring glory to God - when you are a winner.

Learn The Central Truth Of The Word Of God

Somebody said, "Well, God must be trying me to see if I really believe this." That is not true. God knows the thoughts and intents of your heart. (See Hebrews 4:12). He does not have to bring some kind of pressure situation to you in order to find out what you believe. He knows what you believe. If He didn't, He would not be God. He is not the one who brings these things against you.

I realize that in the Old Testament there are many situations that look like God is the author of the trial. I want to emphasize this to you: You need to rightly divide the Word of God. You need to go to the plan of redemption and read it carefully. You need to find out what the Word says about the substitutionary sacrifice of Jesus and what He did for us when He went to Calvary.

A Right Mental Attitude

The substitutionary sacrifice of Jesus is the central truth of the Bible. You need to make everything else that you read in the Bible line up with that central truth.

The moment you read something in the Word that looks as though God brings pressure and trouble against His children, you need to go back to that central truth. If it doesn't line up with the central truth, then you should just put it on the shelf for the time being and ask the Holy Spirit to reveal it to you.

There have been times when I would run across a situation when I was reading in the Old Testament and I have said, "Wait a minute! That blows everything that I have ever learned." And I would say, "Now God, You told me that You were not the one who did that. But right here it says plainly, 'The Lord shall smite thee.'" That was when I went back to the central truth. **And the central truth is: Jesus was smitten (bruised) on my behalf. Jesus bore those things for me.**

The Bible says in Isaiah 53:

Surely he hath borne our griefs, and carried

our sorrows ...he was wounded for our transgressions, he was bruised for our iniquities: the chastisement of our peace was upon him; and with his stripes we are healed.

All we like sheep have gone astray; we have turned everyone to his own way; and the Lord hath laid on him the iniquity of us all ...it pleased the Lord to bruise him; he hath put him to grief... (vv. 4-6, 10).

That is the central truth upon which you can base everything in the Word. If it was the will of God that Jesus be bruised, then it can never be the will of God that you be bruised. If it is God's will that you be bruised, then Jesus was bruised in vain. And if Jesus was bruised in vain, then the substitutionary sacrifice did not work. And if the substitutionary sacrifice did not work, then Romans 10:9-10 has no power. And if Romans 10:9-10 has no power, then you and I are still lost.

That central truth is summed up in four words: **Jesus was our substitute**. Praise God! We can base everything around that truth. Because of what Jesus did at Calvary, God has provided for us a means whereby we can over-

A Right Mental Attitude

come everything that Satan throws at us. God knows that Satan is a spiritual outlaw and that he is out to kill, to steal, and to destroy. And He realizes that you and I can be contacted by him, physically and mentally, in some form. Therefore, God gave us weapons that are not carnal to use to fight against Satan. He has put in our hands the means whereby, regardless of what Satan brings, there is a way of escape.

This is what He is telling us in Peter's writings. God is glorified when we use these weapons and defeat Satan. God doesn't receive glory when we are beaten. Jesus tells us in His teachings just exactly how we can glorify our Father.

If ye abide in me, and my words abide in you, ye shall ask what ye will, and it shall be done unto you. **Herein is my Father glorified, that ye bear much fruit**; So shall ye be my disciples (John 15:7-8).

Notice, He didn't say anything about God receiving glory when we are beaten down and defeated. He said God is glorified when we are full of His Word, and that Word makes us fruitful or productive.

Satan Will Give You The Opportunity To Get Into The Furnace

God realizes that you and I have the opportunity to be contacted by Satan from time to time. So, He has provided a way of escape. Remember that Isaiah 54:17 says: **No weapon formed against thee shall prosper**.

It would not have been a witness of God's power to Nebuchadnezzar if those three young Hebrew men had come out of that furnace with their legs burned and no hair upon their heads. But when they came out on the other side of that furnace glorifying God, it certainly impressed Nebuchadnezzar. In fact, he issued a new decree:

Therefore I make a decree, That every people, nation, and language, which speak any thing amiss against the God of Shadrach, Meshach, and Abednego, shall be cut in pieces, and their houses shall be made a dunghill: because there is no other God that can deliver after this sort (Daniel 3:29).

God is not glorified when His children are

beaten down, beggarly, and suffering. Even though Satan will bring situations to you and try to steal the Word of God out of your heart, you can bring glory to God when you take His Word and resist the devil until he flees. You are a testimony that God's Word works. You are more than a conqueror through Him. You bring glory to God because you approach every situation with a *right mental attitude*.

EIGHT

Two Avenues - Faith And Fear

●●●

When Peter said, W*herefore gird up the loins of your mind, be sober, and hope to the end for the grace that is to be brought unto you at the revelation of Jesus Christ* (1 Peter 1:13), he was implying that you need to have a right mental attitude at all times. You need to think soberly and to have your mind renewed to the Word of God. **As you continue to inject God's Word into your heart, it will produce a very positive mental attitude in you**. Again, I want you to realize that I am not dealing with just the *power of positive thinking*. But if you start thinking about God's Word, you cannot help but think positively.

Somebody said, "Well, why doesn't every Christian think this way?" Because some are putting the wrong thing in their heart.

I said, "Put God's Word in your heart." I didn't say anything about putting religious tradition in your heart. Traditions of men make the Word of God of no effect.

Somebody else might say, "Well, why

A Right Mental Attitude

doesn't every Full Gospel person have a right mental attitude?" The reason is that some of them put the wrong things in their heart.

I said, "Put the Word in your heart." Some "Full Gospel" people have just as many religious traditions in their church as others. I am talking about the power of God's Word. I am not talking about men's traditions, religious ideas, or demoninational doctrines. I am talking about the pure Word of the Living God. **The pure Word of the living God will create a very positive mental attitude**.

A right mental attitude is very important when facing what Peter described as "a trial by fire". If you enter into a trial with a negative attitude, you are going to lose. You won't expect to come out victoriously.

At this point, somebody might be thinking: What are you trying to do, prepare us for trials?

Well, that is not a bad idea. Don't misunderstand me. I am not telling you that you have to go through trials. Some Christians think that God sends trials to perfect us. The trial is not what perfects you. It is what you do with the

Word of God in the midst of a trial that perfects you. Many Christians have been beaten in the trials that Satan brings against them. And it is evident that there is a need for much teaching on this. So, if you want to ask if I am preparing you for a trial, the answer is **yes**!

Thank God, there is a way that you can endure (overcome), and it is through the Word of God.

I have discovered some things about Satan, and I am eager to share them with you. Paul said that we are not ignorant of Satan's devices. I discovered that the more you learn about how the devil operates, the more advantages you will have over him.

Once I was in a seminar in the northwestern part of the United States. As I sat in my room going over the Word and meditating the things that I was going to be preaching in that meeting, Satan began to bring up things to intimidate me. Since this was our first seminar in this city, I didn't know how successful our meeting would be. Some people had taken what used to be a night club and converted it into a Christian restaurant. We were to conduct our meetings in

A Right Mental Attitude

what was formerly the dance hall.

Finally, it was time for our first service and only a handful of people showed up. I thought, *What is going on here*? At about 8:00 o'clock, a couple walked in. The person who was in charge said, "Oh, we have had a struggle here. I tell you, there isn't anyone in this city who believes anything."

I thought, *That's good news*! Then I was told, "There has been a foul-up in the advertising, and it didn't get out."

I thought, *That's two good reports that I have received since I've come in*. That was intimidation from Satan. I did not receive it. I went in there and preached just as though the place was full. The worst thing that I could have done was walk off. That would have destroyed my faith.

The next night was even worse. They had brought in a singing group and scheduled them for the same time that we were scheduled - except they were to be in the smaller dance hall. When I walked into the hall, the three staff members that I had brought with me were there.

"What is going on?" I asked. They told me that the singing group would have meetings in the smaller room. I looked at one of them and asked, "Are you ready to preach?" I was about to go back to the motel when I caught on to what Satan was trying to do. Like the night before, Satan was intimidating me. I was about to destroy my faith and my right mental attitude.

God told me to go in there and preach; to be instant in season and out of season. He did not tell me to preach only if the place was full. He told me to **preach**! We started right on time, and the anointing of God came on me and we had a great time!

I Laughed At The Devil

Between services when I was in my room, I would think about Satan trying to intimidate me, and I would start laughing. He would bring this thought to me: You came all the way from Ft. Worth, Texas, and you brought three men with you. You could have done this meeting by yourself.

I said, "I'm not moved by what I see," and then I would start laughing again. I thought,

A Right Mental Attitude

There is something to this. Here I am laughing at what looks like destruction. Evidently, I must have discovered a truth. I started looking in the Word of God, and I found out what I had gotten hold of, praise God. I started praising God **in** that situation. I realized that Satan was trying to intimidate me.

Here is what the Lord taught me: **Satan's avenue is fear** - the fear of failure, the fear of insecurity, the fear of not having the needs met, the fear of not being accepted, the fear of nobody showing up, and the fear of the meeting being a flop.

Threats And Intimidations Are Not Realities Until They Are Acted Upon

You can apply this to anything that you are doing. I am just talking about a particular meeting. I began to realize that threats and intimidations are not realities until they are acted upon. They are not in manifestation form until you act upon them. Satan will intimidate you through words, actions, or signs. He will give you a sign or indication to back his intimidation. But none of those things can become reality or come into manifestation until you act upon them.

Watch what I am saying. Satan tried to intimidate me with these words: "This meeting is going to be a flop, Jerry. You should not have come here. Nobody will turn out for this meeting. You are wasting your time." I was hearing those words. Then came the signs. We arrived at the meeting at 7:30, and Satan gave me a sign to back his intimidation, a handful of people. The worst thing I could have done was to respond in fear and act on those intimidations, because the moment he could get me to act upon them, they would have become a reality. They would have come into manifestation, and that meeting would have been a flop, a disaster. You see, Satan has a counterfeit for everything that God does.

God's Avenue Is Faith

God also contacts you through words, actions, or signs, and **God wants you to act on what He says**. Then it will come into manifestation. The one who acts on what God says will be blessed in his deeds.

Satan uses intimidation and threats to get us to act upon our fears. Fear will bring things to pass just as faith will. Job said, "That which I greatly feared has come upon me." If you have a fear of failure and are being intimidated or threatened by Satan, there is absolutely no way that he can cause that to become a reality unless you start acting on what he says.

Gloria Copeland once shared with me that she asked the following question: "Father, can the devil do anything that he wants to do, anytime that he gets ready to do it?"

God told her, "If he could do anything he wanted to do, anytime he got ready to do it, then why would he have to deceive you first?" Satan is limited when he can't get you to act on his threats through fear.

Man Is The Establishing Witness

Man stands in a strategic position. He can be contacted by both God and Satan. You might say that man is the *establishing witness*. (See Matthew 18:16; 2 Corinthians 13:1). Satan brings intimidation and threats, and if man acts upon them, they come to pass. God contacts

Two Avenues - Faith and Fear

man through His Word, and if man acts on His Word, it comes to pass. The choice is man's. The devil cannot do anything unless he can first come in and deceive, intimidate, threaten the man, and then get him to fall for it and to act in fear. If he can get man to act in fear, then he has a legal right to cause it to become a reality.

All of us have been through difficult situations which looked as though they had no way out. I would be lying to you if I said I have never been in any difficult situations. But praise be to God for His Word! If it was not for God's Word, I would have failed miserably long ago. There have been times when it seemed as though failure was inevitable. And at times I wasn't too sure if God even knew what I needed. It was pleasing to know that He did know, and He never failed me or let me fall to Satan's attack.

Satan was doing all he could to intimidate me and to prove that there was no help for me. But I thank God that He did what He said He would do. He provided a way of escape.

God always provides a way of escape, but you must approach the trial with a right mental attitude. The only way that you can develop a

A Right Mental Attitude

right mental attitude about it is to **know what the Word says**. If you do not know that God will provide an avenue of escape in every situation, then you will enter that problem with a negative attitude, and Satan will beat you. The Word says in Psalm 34:19, *Many are the afflictions of the righteous; but the Lord delivereth him out of them all.*

Even when the pressure comes, you can think positively, according to what God says in His Word. You can laugh at the devil and say, "Satan, I am not moved by this. Bring what you will, but God will always provide a way of escape. You are not going to defeat me this time. The only way you can do that is if God fails. And He is not going to! God is the great **I AM**. He is on my side, and you can't beat us."

Approach the pressure that Satan is bringing against you with a positive, right mental attitude. That is what Peter means when he says, "Gird up the loins of your mind." In other words, get ready to do something that may be strenuous or difficult. When difficult times come upon you, that is when you, as a believer, should excel. "Word people" should excel when the

Two Avenues - Faith and Fear

pressure is on. That is a tremendous testimony to the world.

Anybody can go through a trial and come out on the other side beaten and worn out. There is a strength that comes to one when he is approaching every situation with a right mental attitude. You can approach each problem through God's avenue of faith and come out victoriously, or you can approach it through Satan's avenue of fear and be defeated. The decision is yours.

NINE

Become Established In Righteousness

•••

*T*he Spirit of God once shared some exciting truths with me as I read the following Scripture passage:

In righteousness shalt thou be established: thou shalt be far from oppression; for thou shalt not fear; and from terror; for it shall not come near thee (Isaiah 54:14).

Now what would that do to your attitude if you began to read those scriptures daily? It would cause you to think positively. This is the Lord, our Redeemer, talking. And he continues in verses 16 and 17.

Behold, I have created the smith that bloweth the coals in the fire, and that bringeth forth an instrument for his work; and I have created the waster to destroy.

No weapon that is formed against thee shall prosper; and every tongue that shall rise against thee in judgment thou shalt condemn.

This is the heritage of the servants of the

A Right Mental Attitude

Lord, and their righteousness is of me, saith the Lord.

There is an important key to victory in those scriptures. He said, "Thou shalt be far from oppression; for thou shalt not fear: and from terror; for it shall not come near thee." When does all of this take place? When you are established in righteousness.

Righteousness is the reality of having right standing with the God of this universe. And the manifestation of that reality is when you know that even in pressure situations, He will never leave you nor forsake you, and He will always provide for you a way of escape. "No weapon formed against you will prosper."

When you are established in your right standing, it will produce in you a positive mental attitude about everything you encounter in this earth. It makes no difference what comes your way; when you know that you have right standing with God, you know that you do not have to compromise. You know that you don't have to worry about whether or not God is going to keep His Word. If God is for you, who can be against you?

Become Established in Righteousness

When you are established in righteousness, oppression does not come near you. **All Christians are not established in righteousness**, even though they are the righteousness of God. (2 Corinthians 5:21). There are many oppressed Christians. Oppression can come to one spiritually, mentally, or physically. Oppression could be defined as "unjust or cruel exercise of power." So, oppression is brought on by an unjust use of power or authority, and Satan is the unjust one who brings oppression to mankind. He has no legal right to do it, but he will do it if you are not established in righteousness. You have opened the door to be oppressed by the unjust one if you give him the authority. God's Word is telling us: "Thou shalt be far from oppression when you are established in righteousness."

He also said, "...for thou shalt not fear, and from terror; for it shall not come near thee." Terror is intense fear caused by intimidations and threats, and the result is dread, dismay, and loss of courage. If all Christians would stop operating in fear, they would conquer every one of their problems.

God said that they (fear, terror, and oppression) shall not come near you. But there is a condition. The condition is: "Thou shalt be established in righteousness." You have to know your rights. You have to know where you stand, and you have to know who you are in Christ Jesus. You need to know and understand how to appropriate the things that God has said. You must learn how to use the weapons that are not carnal but are mighty to the pulling down of Satan's strongholds. You must never forget that God will make a way of escape for you. This will make you a winner and not a failure, because you are the righteousness of God.

Get Mad At The Devil

Ecclesiastes 7:7 says, *Surely oppression maketh a wise man mad*. You need to get mad at your enemy. He wants to intimidate you and to threaten you. He wants to oppress and bring dread, dismay, and lack of courage to you. It is time for you to get mad at the devil. You can get angry at him and your "righteous indignation" will rise. You can resist him with the Word. **When I say get mad at the devil, I mean draw the battle lines and let him know that you refuse to stand by and just allow him to win.** Fight the good fight of faith and wage a good warfare.

I am reminded of a time when I was working with Kenneth Copeland. We were conducting some meetings and there was a stagehand who was a rough-talking, tobacco-chewing guy who later received salvation. He liked Brother Copeland's preaching. When Brother Copeland walked past him one night, the man stopped him and said, "Do you mean to tell me that the devil is the one that caused all my problems?"

"That's him," Brother Copeland answered.

Do you mean to tell me that I have been going through this for all these years, and it was the devil that did it?"

Brother Copeland said, "That's right." The man didn't know any other way to express his anger, so he just started "cussing" the devil. We told him that is not the way to resist the devil. We started teaching him the Word, and he began to get hold of it. "Cussing" the devil won't hurt him; that's his language. But, praise God, speaking the Word will cut him like a twoedged sword.

The Bible says that when the wise man is oppressed, he gets mad. He begins to lean on his

A Right Mental Attitude

right standing with God and say, "I don't have to put up with this. I am the righteousness of God." Once you get stubborn with your faith and push your righteousness to its limit, there is nothing that the devil can do to stop you. You are approaching the problem with a right mental attitude. You know who you are in Christ, and you know your rights. You are established in righteousness. You cannot fail.

TEN

The Sacrifice Of Joy

●●●

If you give place to fear, you allow oppression to come. If you continue to act on fear, an unreasoning state of panic will spread quickly and lead to irrational action. Once you are in a state of panic, it will spread so quickly that you will not have time to collect your thoughts, and you will end up doing something that you should not have done. That is exactly what the devil wants you to do.

You can stop panic in its tracks if you will offer the sacrifice of joy. You may say, "The sacrifice of joy! What do you mean?"

Let's go to Psalm 27 and see what David said about it.

The Lord is my light and my salvation; whom shall I fear? the Lord is the strength of my life; of whom shall I be afraid?

When the wicked, even mine enemies and my foes, came upon me to eat up my flesh, they stumbled and fell.

A Right Mental Attitude

Though an host should encamp against me, my heart shall not fear: though war should rise against me, in this will I be confident.

One thing have I desired of the Lord, that will I seek after; that I may dwell in the house of the Lord all the days of my life, to behold the beauty of the Lord, and to enquire in his temple.

For in the time of trouble he shall hide me in his pavilion: in the secret of his tabernacle shall he hide me; he shall set me up upon a rock.

And now shall mine head be lifted up above mine enemies round about me: therefore will I offer in his tabernacle sacrifices of joy: I will sing, yea, I will sing praises unto the Lord (vv. 1-6).

Notice the phrase, "sacrifices of joy." You might think that the least opportune time to be joyful is when you are being tried by Satan. When you are under pressure and the circumstances are all running contrary to God's Word, and it seems as though everything is against you; **this is when you should offer sacrifices of joy**.

David was talking about a right mental

attitude when he said, "...My head shall be lifted up above mine enemies round about me; *therefore will I offer in his tabernacle sacrifices of joy*. I will sing, yea, I will sing praises unto the Lord" (v.6).

David continues, "*Hear, O Lord, when I cry with my voice: have mercy also upon me, and answer me*" (v.7). He was talking about what he does when he has the opportunity to be oppressed and when his enemies are coming against him. He was talking about what to do when experiencing hard times. I want you to notice what David said that he was going to do. He was approaching these problems based upon his covenant with God. He had a very *positive mental attitude*.

He said, "I'll tell you what I am going to do about all this. I am going to praise God and offer sacrifices of joy. And God will hear me and answer me" (author's paraphrase).

Does that sound to you as though David was worried about his enemies? Does that sound like he expected failure? No! He said, "I'll tell you what I am going to do. I am going to offer sacrifices of joy."

A Right Mental Attitude

I love this Scripture passage because I understand now what Brother Kenneth E. Hagin was talking about when he would say, "I am going to laugh at the devil."

I used to think, *How in the world can a person go around laughing when it looks like failure is at hand*? He knew how to apply this great biblical principle. He was offering the sacrifice of joy. Well, now I know how, and oh, does it ever make the devil angry!

If you will begin by offering the sacrifice of joy, it won't be long until it will no longer be a sacrifice. The joy of the Lord will overcome you. The praise of God and the Word of God will begin to flow out of your mouth and your mouth will be filled with laughter and joy. God will hear and answer you. And He will see to it, as you lean on your right standing with Him, that trouble will be far from you.

Approach Every Problem With A Right Mental Attitude

You may ask, "How should I think when trouble comes?"

The Sacrifice of Joy

When trouble comes to you, pick up your Bible and read Isaiah 54:14-17 and say it, and say it, and say it, and say it. Then turn to Psalm 27 and say it, and say it, and say it. Then begin to act upon it. The rest is up to God. You are not the one who is responsible for bringing the Word to pass; God is. Start out by praising Him for your deliverance, and if you have to, offer the **sacrifice of joy**.

Somebody said, "What am I supposed to do, just praise God *for* this situation?"

No. Just praise God and thank Him that He has provided a way of escape for you. *You do not praise God for the trial.* **You praise God for your deliverance**. Praise God for the power of His Word. Praise God for the name of Jesus. Praise God that you are a winner, and that He hears and answers your prayers. As you begin praising God as a sacrifice, you will finally end up praising Him because joy has come in its fullness.

You Do Not Pretend That The Problem Does Not Exist

Laughing at the devil or offering sacrifices

A Right Mental Attitude

of joy are not ways to pretend that you don't have any problems. These are reality in its highest form. These are some things that you can do about the problem. Some people will just mentally shut themselves away from the problem and pretend that it does not exist. This is not what I am talking about. Somewhere down the road, they are going to have to come back to reality, and the problem will still be there.

Jesus said, "Thy word is truth." God's Word is reality. **When you acquire a right mental attitude about every situation based upon the Word of God, then you are actually putting yourself in the position where God is able to provide an avenue of escape**. You are not pretending that the problem doesn't exist, but you are actually applying the spiritual power that will cause it to depart far from you.

How far is *far*? The Bible says that Jesus is *far* above all principalities, and power, and might, and dominion, and every name that has been named. How far do you suppose that is?

Well, however far Jesus is above demonic activity, that is how *far* oppression, fear, and terror should be from you. When you have a right mental attitude and offer the sacrifice of joy, your problems will begin to be *far* from you.

In The Midst Of Trials, Bring Glory To God

You will remember that Peter talked about bringing glory and honor to God in the *midst* of some uncomfortable situations. He termed them *manifold temptations* in 1 Peter 1:6. Peter is implying that even in the midst of heaviness and manifold temptations, we are to bring glory and honor to God.

The only way you can do that when you are being tempted or tested is to approach it with a proper mental attitude. And unless you have a right mental attitude, when the pressure comes, you will be consumed by it.

Shadrach, Meshach, and Abednego were tested with heaviness in a fiery furnace. They went into that furnace with a proper mental attitude in spite of how things looked. They confessed and agreed together: "We will not bow our knee; and if we do go through this furnace, our God is able to deliver us."

A Right Mental Attitude

They were prepared for whatever might come. Many Christians misunderstand, and they will say, "God did that to them because He was not too sure if they would really stand; He was trying their faith."

Again I say, **no**! God does not have to put you in a furnace or cause a flood to come your way to find out what you will do in a certain situation or how you will react. He knows every thought and intent of your heart. It is Satan who is not too sure about you.

You may ask, "Does Satan know what is in my mind?" He only knows what you allowed him to put in your mind. *He does not know the thought and intent of your heart.*

The New Testament says, "Let no man say when he is temped, I am tempted of God " (James 1:13). If you are going to be victorious, then you must learn to follow the instructions in the Word.

If the pressure comes and you say, "I guess God did this to teach me something," then there is no way that you will come through that trial victoriously. You have played right into the devil's hand by thinking that God is part of your problem. This is the wrong kind of attitude. You must know that Satan is the tempter and that God is the deliverer.

ELEVEN

Become Strong-Willed

●●●

For if by one man's offence death reigned by one; much more they which receive abundance of grace and of the gift of righteousness shall reign in life by one, Jesus Christ (Romans 5:17).

If you have accepted Jesus as your Lord, then you are the righteousness of God. Because of this, you have a right to reign in life. For many Christians, life is reigning over them because they have not had their minds renewed to God's Word. When adversity comes, they don't have the will to win, simply because they don't know that they have a right to win. Christians who know their rights in Christ are strong-willed people. They are as Paul described in his writings: "...having done all to stand (they) stand therefore..."

Some Christians still have a tendency to think that they are unworthy, no good, and "just an old worm." They desperately need to hear the truth about becoming established in righteousness.

Some Christians still think that God wants

them to be sick and diseased. They, too, need to have their minds renewed to God's Word. When symptoms come, they do not have the will to resist them because they think that God is the one who sent them. **God is the healer!** *People who don't know the Word are people without restraint when pressure comes.*

You should know that sickness and disease are not from God. You should know that they are of Satan. You should become so established in the Word that nobody can convince you that God is the one who puts sickness and disease on you.

Just as you need to become established in God's will for your health, you need to be established in how to overcome the trials and temptations that Satan will bring against you. As a Christian, you need to face up to the fact that you are still in the world, even though you are not of the world. Therefore, because Satan is in the world, he has the ability to contact you from time to time.

You do not have to be defeated or destroyed by those contacts. By acting on the Word, you can come through every problem unshaken. (Luke 6:46-49).

Please do not get the idea that I am saying everyone must have trials. What I am saying is this: It is time that Christians learn how to gird up the loins of their mind when pressure comes; then they can overcome it.

Because many Christians have not been taught properly, they just accept what Satan brings to them, and they say, "This must be God's will. There is nothing I can do about it."

If the Bible says that you can do all things through Christ Jesus who strengthens you and that you are more than a conqueror, then I ask you: What can Satan possibly do to defeat you?

Christians Should Become Strong-Willed

Many times we teach a lot on the spirit of man and fail to teach enough on the soul (the mind, will, and emotions) of man. Of course, man is a spirit and we need to know more about educating, developing, and perfecting the spirit of man. But the Bible also emphasizes the

A Right Mental Attitude

importance of the renewing of the mind and having a willingness of mind. Do you remember the Scripture that says, "Thou will keep him in perfect peace whose mind is stayed on thee" (Isaiah 26:3)? God is interested in you doing something with your mind also.

Faith Is Not A Mental Exercise It Is A Spiritual Force

There is a danger in just dealing with the mind alone. Some people get off into an area of only applying mental power. That is wrong. You must realize that faith is not a mental exercise but a spiritual force. If you live by faith, you will develop a right mental attitude. You will "think positive". I will say this again: The power of positive thinking is limited if it is not based on God's Word. If you get your mind renewed to the Word, there is absolutely no way that you can keep from thinking positively because all the promises of God are *yea and in Him amen*. That means, *affirmative and so be it*.

When there is pressure, you should get ready to do something that may be difficult. It may demand discipline. A real "Word person" is a *strong-willed* person.

Become Strong-Willed

When you become *strong-willed* on the Word of God, you will say like the song, "I shall not be moved. I'm just like a tree planted by the river." That is the voice of a *strong-willed* person who knows where he stands in God's Word. He is determined that, if anybody moves, it will just have to be the devil.

This kind of attitude does not come to you overnight. You must feed on God's Word day and night until you know that you know that you know.

Many people are inspired by the message of faith. It sounds good to them, and they run out and say, "Bless God, I am going to talk like that. I shall not be moved." Let me warn you of this: Don't try to live on something that is not a revelation to you personally. But when the Word is deeply rooted in your heart, then stand your ground until the devil backs off.

When you base your confession on the authority of God's Word and are deeply rooted in it, you can say, "I shall not be moved," and it will come forth with joy and assurance. You will know that you cannot be moved. You have become strong-willed in the Word of God.

A Right Mental Attitude

Don't Allow Your Will To Become Passive

When Peter told us to gird up the loins of our mind, he was saying, "Get ready to do something that may be difficult." The reason that it may be difficult is that there is a lack of discipline on your part. If you lack discipline, your will may also become passive. A good example of someone whose will has become passive is the example that Solomon used in Proverbs 22:13. *The slothful man saith, There is a lion without, I shall be slain in the streets.* This man accepted defeat when it was not inevitable. Many Christians are this way today.

I used to have a wrong mental attitude about everything. Then I realized that it **takes determination, diligence, and discipline to live by God's system**.

It took time for me to change the way I thought. But, praise God, the day finally came when God's thoughts became my thoughts. His Word renewed my mind and caused me to have the **will to win**.

You have to hear the Word, meditate the

Become Strong-Willed

Word, and act on the Word. As your mind lines up with the Word of God, you will become strong-willed. With a renewed mind, a right mental attitude, a strong will, and faith in your heart, you are totally unlimited in what you can accomplish in this earth for the glory of God.

TWELVE

Greatly Rejoicing - An Aid To A Right Mental Attitude

●●●

Wherein ye greatly rejoice, though now for a season if need be, ye are in heaviness through manifold temptations (1 Peter 1:6).

If you are faced with a crisis, then you must immediately gird up the loins of your mind. You must not only prepare to release your faith, but you must prepare to do something mental: to look at the problem with a positive attitude.

How?

The first thing you have to understand is this: Manifold temptations, testings, trials, and pressures do not come from God. If you look at it any other way, your mental attitude will be negative. Secondly, manifold temptations, testings, trials and pressures are not designed by God to perfect you. **The Word is the perfecter of the Church**. *All scripture is given by inspiration of God, and is profitable for doctrine, for reproof, for correction, for instruction in righteousness* (2 Timothy 3:16).

Get this out of your thinking immediately:

A Right Mental Attitude

"Well, all things work together for the good of those that love God, and are called according to His purpose." Somebody said, "Well, that's what the Bible says." Yes, but you are taking scriptures out of context. What you are actually saying is this: "Come what may, it is of God, and I suppose it is for my good." You can take scriptures out of their setting and destroy your faith. How can you trust God to deliver you if you think that He is the one who created your problem?

The proper mental attitude says, "This is not of God; it is Satan who comes immediately to steal the Word from my heart (Mark 4:14-20). It is Satan who comes to kill, to steal, and to destroy (John 10:10). I am girding up the loins of my mind; I am prepared to release my faith, to stand strong on the Word, and to approach this problem with a proper mental attitude. I fully expect my God to deliver me." Next you should begin to rejoice and praise God for the victory.

The apostle Paul said in Philippians 4:4, *Rejoice in the Lord alway: and again I say, Rejoice*. And Peter said, "Wherein ye greatly rejoice..." Rejoicing absolutely blows the devil's plan. All Satan can do is make threats. He cannot defeat you if you will not act in fear. When he tries to intimidate you, just stand up and rejoice.

"At Destruction And Famine Thou Shalt Laugh..."

Let's not get off into false teaching that says, "Praise God *for* the problem." No. You do not thank God *for* the problem. Job 5:22 gives some insight into God's attitude toward that kind of thinking: *At destruction and famine thou shalt laugh.* You cannot laugh at a problem until you know what God says about it. God is telling you not to laugh and rejoice because of the situation but to *rejoice because of the answer to it*. The answer can be found in the Word.

We read in Habakkuk 3:17: *Although the fig tree shall not blossom, neither shall fruit be in the vines; the labour of the olive shall fail, and fields shall yield no meat; the flock shall be cut off from the fold, and there shall be no herd in the stalls.*

Many Christians stop reading at this point and begin to identify with failure. But that is not what he is saying. We need to read on. He says,

A Right Mental Attitude

"Yet..." "Yet" means that he is not through talking. *Yet I will rejoice in the Lord; I will joy in the God of my salvation. The Lord God is my strength, and he will make my feet like hinds' feet, and he will make me to walk upon mine high places* (vv. 18-19). This is the proper mental attitude about famine and destruction.

The man is saying, "I have a proper mental attitude. Even if these things do happen, it makes no difference. I will rejoice in the Lord. He is my salvation. And He will make my feet like hinds' feet, and I will jump right over the problem.

You do not overcome destruction and famine by isolating yourself from the problem and getting over into some kind of fantasy-land, pretending that the problem doesn't exist.

You face the truth. And Jesus said, "Thy Word is truth" (John 17:17). The word "truth" means "the highest form of reality that exists". It is not what somebody else says about it. God's Word is truth, and He said, "Thou shalt laugh at famine and destruction."

When you rejoice in the Lord, He becomes

your strength. He will make your feet like hinds' feet, and He will make you walk in high places. Because you have the assurance that, even though the pressure is on you, you can laugh at famine. You can laugh when it looks as though things are not working. You can rejoice in the Lord because He is your strength.

You will remember in the book of Job that Satan came to destroy everything that Job owned. God was the One who made him wealthy. Job was the richest man in all the East. If you read the entire book, you know that Job was blessed with twice everything that he lost. God was talking to Job when he said, "Thou shalt laugh at famine and destruction." Many people think that God brought these problems on Job, but He didn't. God told him how to overcome them.

Many Christians Don't Know How To Laugh At Their Problems

To be honest, you will never be able to laugh and rejoice in the face of a crisis until you learn to gird up the loins of your mind. And you cannot gird up the loins of your mind until you know what the Word says concerning your problems. Once you know what the Word says, you

A Right Mental Attitude

can offer the sacrifice of joy even in the midst of adversity.

Joy brings laughter. It creates laughter. But if you do not know what the Word says about joy, you will never be able to experience it.

Think of a situation that you are facing at the present time. Something that is most difficult. Possibly, you are believing God for finances, for healing, or for deliverance from a severe problem. Stop right now and begin to offer the sacrifice of joy. **Now**, laugh. Laugh. Laugh! If you have a problem laughing, that's a good indication that you have not been trained to laugh at destruction and famine. You have been trained, perhaps, to sit down and cry and indulge in self-pity. You may be crying out for someone to sympathize with you. *Sympathy never finds a solution. Sympathy only sees the problem as hopeless.* Jesus did not move in sympathy. He moved with compassion. *Compassion finds the answer and acts.*

Once you have trained yourself to laugh at destruction and famine, you will have the assurance in your heart that, regardless of what Satan attempts to do, you can say, "God is my strength, and He makes my feet like hinds' feet. This is just another opportunity to prove that Jesus is Lord and the Word of God works."

Learn To Laugh With God At The Devil

I had to train myself to have a right mental attitude. Now when pressure comes, I just join with God and laugh at what the devil tries to do. Did you know that God is laughing at Satan? Well, He is. Read Psalm 2:4: *He that sitteth in the heavens shall laugh.* Also, Psalm 37:13: *The Lord shall laugh at him, for he seeth that his day is coming.*

It is absolutely enjoyable to learn to laugh at defeat.

Someone might say, "Is that all you do, just laugh?"

No. I act on the Word as the Spirit of God shows me, and then I stand fast until I win. I have the opportunity to hear Satan's negative thoughts. Sometimes the thought would come to my mind: *You know you will never have the money that you need.* When that thought comes, I can either

A Right Mental Attitude

cast it down or dwell upon it. If I start dwelling on it, Satan will paint the most awful picture of failure that you can imagine. But at that moment, I begin to laugh at the devil. I have learned to be quick about this. I just laugh and laugh and continually speak the Word of God.

The devil says, "What are you laughing about? You must not have heard me."

I say, "Oh, yes, I heard you, and that is exactly what I am laughing at. You keep telling me that I cannot win, but God keeps telling me that I can. Who would *you* believe?"

I have learned that Satan's lies cannot come to pass in my life unless I act on them through fear.

Isaiah 64:5 says, *Thou meetest him that rejoiceth and worketh righteousness*. When you learn to follow these instructions, God promises that He will meet you. Proverbs 17:22 says, *A merry heart doeth good like a medicine*. You can laugh at the signs of destruction. God will meet them that rejoice. Learning to laugh will do you good. Rejoicing and laughing at the problem will help you to get your mind off the

Greatly Rejoicing - An Aid to a Right Mental Attitude

problem and on the Word. You can rejoice in the face of that problem. You can approach it with faith in your heart and assurance from the Word that God is going to get involved in this with you, and the outcome will be victory.

The Bible says that I am seated with Christ in heavenly places. Do you know what Jesus' attitude is? He is fully expecting His enemies to be made his footstool. He is far above all principality, might, dominion, and every name that is named. The Bible says that God sits on His throne and laughs at His enemies. God laughs at Satan. Well, I am seated with Him and I can expect the same results. That's why I can laugh.

Have you ever noticed that when you start laughing with somebody you become friendly? You do not stand far off from one another. The first thing you know, you are embracing one another and patting each other on the back and saying, "I'll tell you, that is the funniest thing that I have ever seen!"

When God said, "I will meet him that rejoices," He was saying, "I will get in there and

A Right Mental Attitude

join you in your laughter." You and God can have a good laugh about the devil.

You owe it to yourself to become established in God's Word. Find out what the Word says about every situation in your life. Then you will have the assurance that God will deliver you from every problem. As this becomes a reality in your heart, regardless of what Satan tries to do, joy will rise up on the inside of you because you know that God is on your side. He will make your feet like hinds' feet. He will strengthen you, and there is nothing that Satan can do to shake you.

Rejoice in the Lord alway: and again I say, rejoice.

Rejoice! God will meet you.

Rejoice! Get your mind off the problem and on the answer. Gird up the loins of your mind.

The battle is the Lord's and the victory is yours!

Dr. Jerry Savelle is a noted author, evangelist, and teacher who travels extensively throughout the United States, Canada, and overseas. He is president of Jerry Savelle Ministries, a ministry of many outreaches devoted to meeting the needs of believers all over the world.

Well-known for his balanced Biblical teaching, Dr. Savelle has conducted seminars, crusades and conventions for over twenty years as well as holding meetings in local churches and fellowships. He is being used to help bridge the gap between the traveling ministry and the local church. In these meetings he is able to encourage and assist pastors in perfecting the saints for the work of the ministry. He is in great demand today because of his inspiring message of victory and faith and his accurate and entertaining illustrations from the Bible. He teaches the uncompromising Word of God with a power and an authority that is exciting, but with a love that delivers the message directly to the spirit man.

When Jerry was 12 years old, God spoke to his heart as he was watching the healing ministry of Oral Roberts on television. God told Jerry that He was calling him into the ministry. Some years later, Jerry made Jesus Christ the Lord of his life and since that time has been moving in the light of that calling.

Dr. Savelle is the founder of Overcoming Faith Churches of Kenya, and the missions outreach of his ministry extends to over 50 different countries around the world. His ministry also delivers the powerful message of God's Word across the United States through the JSM Prison Ministry Outreach.

Dr. Savelle has authored a number of books and has an extensive cassette teaching tape ministry. Thousands of books, tapes, and videos are distributed around the world each year through Jerry Savelle Ministries.

For a complete list of tapes, books and videos by Jerry Savelle, write:

**Jerry Savelle Ministries
P. O. Box 748
Crowley, TX 76036**